I NEED TO
TRUST IN GOD

GOD AND ME

I NEED TO
TRUST IN GOD

Joel and Mary Beeke

Illustrated by Cassandra Clark

Reformation Heritage Books
Grand Rapids, Michigan

I Need to Trust in God
© 2021 by Joel and Mary Beeke

Reformation Heritage Books
3070 29th St. SE
Grand Rapids, MI 49512
616-977-0889
orders@heritagebooks.org
www.heritagebooks.org

Printed in China
21 22 23 24 25 26/10 9 8 7 6 5 4 3 2 1

Library of Congress Cataloging-in-Publication Data

Names: Beeke, Joel R., 1952- author. | Beeke, Mary, author. | Clark, Cassandra, illustrator.
Title: I need to trust in God / Joel and Mary Beeke ; illustrated by Cassandra Clark.
Description: Grand Rapids, Michigan : Reformation Heritage Books, 2021. | Series: God and me | Audience: Ages 4–7
Identifiers: LCCN 2021002919 | ISBN 9781601788696 (hardcover)
Subjects: LCSH: Sin—Christianity—Juvenile literature. | Salvation—Christianity—Juvenile literature. | Trust in God—Christianity—Juvenile literature.
Classification: LCC BT715 .B36 2021 | DDC 234/.23—dc23
LC record available at https://lccn.loc.gov/2021002919

For additional Reformed literature, request a free book list from Reformation Heritage Books at the above regular or email address.

MEMORY VERSE

"Repent, and be converted, that your sins
may be blotted out" (Acts 3:19).

Caleb and Sophie raced outside. Their new swing set and sandbox waited for them.

Sophie made sand pies for her dolls.
Caleb climbed the wall.

"Who can go higher on the swing?"

"Let's go on the see-saw!"

"Let me down! Stop bumping me!"

"It's not my fault you fell."

"I'm telling Mom."

"You always do that;
you're just a cry-baby!"

Supper didn't taste so good. Caleb's
heart felt heavy.

"I wasn't nice to Sophie. I made Sophie fall."

"God, I'm very sorry. I'm full of sin. Please forgive me. Lord, help me to trust Jesus to save me. For Jesus's sake. Amen."

"Caleb, we are so happy to hear you have repented of your sin and want to put your trust in Jesus Christ alone for salvation," Caleb's Dad said. "The Holy Spirit can help you do that by His power in you. The Bible says that when you truly believe on the Lord Jesus Christ, you have true faith, and you will be saved."

TALK ABOUT IT

1. What will we learn to hate when we have true faith?

2. Who will we learn to trust when we have true faith?

Note to parents: Explain to your children that faith involves three acts: to truly know God, to agree with what He says in His Word about Himself and about us, and to trust in His Son alone for salvation. We have no ability to save ourselves. Jesus alone can save us by His death on the cross and by His perfect life of obedience. God's gift of grace enables us to repent of our sins and to trust in Jesus Christ who died on the cross to take the punishment for sinners like us.